Environmental Issues
by Peggy Hapke Lewis

TABLE OF CONTENTS

PAGE	TITLE
1	Environmental Quiz
2	The Greenhouse Effect
3	Slowing Global Warming
4	What Is Ozone?
5	The Tree of Life
6	Trees as Buffers
7	Tropical Rain Forests
8	Gifts from the Rain Forest
9	"Save the Rain Forest" T-Shirt
10	Endangered Species
11	Oil Spills
12	Space Junk
13	The Truth About Trash
14	U.S. Recycling Report Card
15	Recycling Rangers
16	The Earth's Friend or Foe?
17	Smart Shopping for a Better World
18	Save Our Soil
19	Creating Compost
20	Environmental Jobs
21	Energy Store
22	The Wonders of Water
23	It's a Start
24	What Can One Person Do?
25	Environmental Sentences
26	Environment Crossword Puzzle
27	Environmental Glossary
28	Environmental Glossary (continued)

    The activities in this book are designed to give students a heightened awareness of the impact they can have in protecting and improving the environment. Many of the pages are appropriate for use with small groups or with individual students.

    This book works well in conjunction with research projects on the various topics. Opportunities for creative writing and problem solving are plentiful, and many of the pages include interdisciplinary activities using math, art, social studies, and other subjects.

Answers and Suggested Activities

Page 1
This page may be used as a pretest at the beginning of a study of environmental issues and then again at the end as a posttest.
Wording for answers 1 through 7 may vary slightly.
1. air, water, plants, land, and animals around us
2. the protective barrier of gas in the atmosphere which screens out most of the harmful ultraviolet rays from the sun
3. the increasing temperature of the earth resulting from an increase in the gases that cause the greenhouse effect
4. anything that contaminates air, water, or soil and causes harm to living things
5. an area used for dumping solid waste products
6. the way the earth is heated (Gases trapped in the air allow the sun to warm the earth and then keep the heat from escaping.)
7. the burning or cutting down of trees without replanting (This leaves land vulnerable to erosion and destroys trees which produce the oxygen people breathe.)
8. False
9. False
10. False
11. False
12. False
13. True
14. False
15. False

Page 2
1. Answers will vary slightly but should include the idea that the gases in the air allow the sun's heat in and trap it to warm the earth.
2. Answers may include stopping deforestation, using solar energy rather than fossil fuels, recycling, carpooling, walking rather than driving when possible, etc.

A good experiment for showing students the greenhouse effect is to place a thermometer inside a glass jar and cover the opening with plastic wrap. Place another thermometer in a similar jar, but punch holes in the plastic wrap. Place both containers in the sun. Let students record the temperatures inside each.

Page 3
1. Answers will vary but could include changes in weather patterns, farming, water levels, etc.
2. Answers will vary but may include the following:
   A. Driving electric cars   C. Composting
   B. Recycling   D. Using solar heat
3. Answers will vary.

Page 4
1. A decrease in ozone may allow the sun's harmful ultraviolet rays to cause skin and eye damage. Too much ozone causes smog that is harmful to living things and corrosive to some surfaces.
2. Students' diagrams will vary. A diagram showing an increase in ozone should show a buildup of gases. A diagram showing a decrease in ozone should show harmful ultraviolet rays reaching the earth.

Page 5
1. Tree roots keep soil from eroding. Shade from trees cools animals, homes, and yards. Trees provide homes for many animals. Trees provide lumber, paper, etc.
2. It is important that forests are replaced so that there will be trees in the future. However, replanting forests will not keep the amount of carbon dioxide the same. Older, larger trees use much more carbon dioxide than do younger, smaller trees.

Page 6
Answers will vary for questions 1 and 2.
3. A buffer is something that protects something else from a strong force.
4. If fish and wildlife ingest the pollutants they could die. Also, pollutants can kill or damage the food that fish and wildlife eat.
5. Tree roots dig deep into the ground and prevent the soil from being washed or blown away.
6. Answers will vary.

Page 7
1. Answers will vary. Possible answers: rain forests are home to half the world's animal and plant species. They also provide us with medicines, clean the air, and prevent erosion.
2. Answers will vary. Possible answers: destruction of the rain forests could cause the loss of animal and plant species and sources for new medicines; damage to the atmosphere; flooding; and erosion.

If possible, ask a local expert on the rain forest to come in and speak to the class. A botanical garden may be able to send resource material to you and your class if you request it.

Page 8

R	Q	X	C	Q	A	D	F	E	R	W	A	I	E	P	S
Y	W	Z	U	W	S	S	M	E	D	I	C	I	N	E	S
I	E	A	N	C	O	F	F	E	E	O	R	U	A	P	D
O	B	S	D	E	D	A	G	Z	T	I	E	L	I	P	F
K	A	P	E	A	N	U	T	S	Y	A	O	T	R	E	G
F	N	D	R	R	M	O	I	S	T	F	L	O	O	R	H
D	A	F	S	T	F	Z	H	Z	L	U	P	L	M	S	J
S	N	G	T	Y	G	P	I	N	E	A	P	P	L	E	S
C	A	N	O	P	Y	X	J	X	M	X	U	O	Z	A	K
A	S	H	R	U	H	C	O	C	O	N	U	T	S	I	L
S	R	J	Y	I	J	C	J	C	N	E	L	A	U	E	M
H	T	K	V	O	K	V	K	V	S	C	O	I	N	U	N
E	Y	L	C	I	N	N	A	M	O	N	V	B	E	O	T
W	U	P	B	P	L	B	L	B	U	Z	L	X	C	V	B
S	I	O	N	M	M	N	M	N	K	L	N	M	L	K	J

© 1999 McDONALD PUBLISHING CO.   ii   ENVIRONMENTAL ISSUES

Page 9
1. 37,500
2. 3,750

Consider working with an art teacher to create designs on plain T-shirts the students bring from home.

Page 10
1. Answers will vary but may include the fact that many people earn a living in the lumber industry and that people use lumber in many ways.
2. Answers will vary but may include the fact that every species is part of a food chain and the loss of even one creature can upset the balance of nature.

Page 11
Answers will vary.

Have groups share their ideas for ways to prevent future oil spills. One idea presently being considered is putting double hulls on tankers. Also, if ships could be navigated away from dangerous areas it would help reduce the occurrence of oil spills. Finding a cleaner, safer source of energy would be ideal.

Page 12
1. Answers will vary but may include the fact that some objects are left behind by astronauts, and others result from launching items into space.
2. Drawings will vary.
3. Answers should include plans for trash produced on the space station and plans to avoid space junk.
4. Scientists may try to track objects to avoid them. They could also build a shield for the space station's protection.
5. Answers will vary.

Page 13
1. Answers will vary but should work out to seventeen trees saved for each ton of paper recycled.
2. Three hours times the number of cans used in each family.
3. 360,000 pounds
4. 10,000 pounds

Remaining answers will vary.

Page 14
Grades will vary but should be justified.

Page 15
1. Answers will vary. Help students to see that mandatory programs would be unnecessary if each person would do his or her part in protecting the environment.
2. Parts of old cars, used motor oil, furniture, toys, books, cans, apple cores, bikes, and bottles can all either be recycled, reused, or composted.

Choose two students to be Recycling Rangers. Have them look around the classroom and make a report about what can be recycled, reused, or conserved. Suggest that students examine their home recycling efforts.

Page 16
1. Answers will vary.
2. Answers will vary.
3. Answers will vary.
4. It is often cheaper to buy in large quantities, and buying in larger quantities often reduces the amount of packaging waste produced.
5. Take your own string or canvas shopping bags to the grocery store.
6. Buy fruits and vegetables from display bins and not those packaged in plastic and paper.
7. Some restaurants have bins for sorting paper from plastic trash. Others may provide such bins if customers request them.
8. Give them to charitable organizations, pass them on to younger brothers or sisters, sell them at a yard sale.
9. Cancel subscriptions no one reads. Share a subscription with a friend or neighbor. Go to the library each week or month to read the magazine. Cancel unwanted catalogs.
10. Use products made from recycled paper. Use cloth towels and napkins instead of paper, etc.

Page 17
The Wasters <u>left all the lights on in the house</u> as they piled into the car. They were <u>driving to the grocery store four blocks away</u>. Mrs. Waster pushed the cart through the produce aisle, tossing in a <u>package of tomatoes</u>. Mr. Waster bought three kinds of bagels and <u>put each in a separate bag</u>. Junior Waster picked out some <u>paper plates and plastic utensils</u> for his upcoming birthday party. Then he picked up his favorite <u>individually wrapped cheese slices</u> and took them to the cart. Sissie Waster bought <u>six tiny cans</u> of tuna. She knew it would take three larger cans to make one meal, but she liked the little cans. The Wasters loaded up on <u>paper towels and napkins</u> and then paid for the groceries. They all helped load the <u>paper grocery bags</u> into the car and headed for home.

In the friendly version of this story, the family would turn off the lights to save electricity and walk to the nearby store to save gas. They would buy tomatoes without packaging and use one bag for the bagels. They would avoid using paper plates and plastic utensils and purchase cheese slices that are wrapped together. They would buy large cans of tuna to reduce the waste created by the cans, use cloth towels and napkins when possible, and bring cloth or string bags to the store to haul the groceries home.

Page 18
1. A. contour plowing
   B. terracing
2. Answers will vary but may include turning off the water when it's not in use or filling the dishwasher completely before running it.
3. Answers will vary but may include plowing and planting in circles rather than rows, or planting windbreaks of some kind.

Page 19
1. false
2. true
3. true
4. true
5. false
6. true
7. false
8. Students should circle the following materials: fallen leaves, coffee grounds, beans, lettuce, grass clippings, twigs, hay, and tree bark.

Page 20
Answers will vary.

Page 21
Answers will vary.

Page 22
1. Answers will vary.
2. The first pie chart should show 3% freshwater and 97% saltwater. The second pie chart should show 75% frozen freshwater and 25% usable freshwater.

Page 23
Students' listed items will vary.

Page 24
Answers and posters will vary.
As extension activities, you may wish to have students write a grant to improve the environment in their community.

Page 25
Sentences and speeches will vary.

Page 26

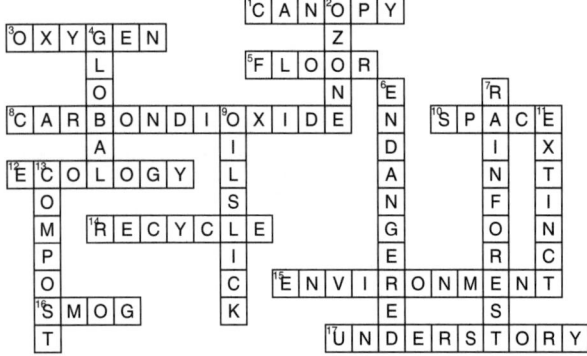

Pages 27 and 28
This glossary can be used during a unit on environmental issues as well as for evaluation purposes. Definitions and spellings of glossary words may be assigned and later tested by essay and/or matching tests. You may decide, after using page 1 as a posttest, to alter the activity on page 28 so that students write about topics you suggest.

NOTES

Name _____

Environmental Quiz

Complete this page to find out how much you already know about the environment.

In your own words, write a definition for each of the following:

1. environment _____
_____

2. ozone layer _____
_____

3. global warming _____
_____

4. pollution _____
_____

5. landfill _____
_____

6. greenhouse effect _____
_____

7. deforestation _____
_____

Read the following statements, then circle true *or* false.

8. An effective solution for getting rid of trash would be to send it into outer space.	TRUE	FALSE
9. If an oil spill dumps millions of gallons into the ocean on the other side of the world, it does not concern us.	TRUE	FALSE
10. The rain forest is valuable mostly for its beauty.	TRUE	FALSE
11. The world would be better off without the greenhouse effect.	TRUE	FALSE
12. If we run out of oil in our country, we can always get more by drilling wells.	TRUE	FALSE
13. Ultraviolet rays are damaging to human skin.	TRUE	FALSE
14. Composting at home is a good way to get rid of old cans and bottles.	TRUE	FALSE
15. Recycling has completely eliminated the problem of limited landfill space.	TRUE	FALSE

© 1999 McDONALD PUBLISHING CO.   ENVIRONMENTAL ISSUES

Name _____

The Greenhouse Effect

When scientists speak of the **"greenhouse effect"** they are talking about the way gases such as carbon dioxide and methane trap enough of the sun's heat to warm our planet. The gases act like the sheets of glass in a greenhouse. They allow the rays of the sun in and then hold the heat inside.

In a greenhouse, the trapping of the sun's heat allows gardeners to grow plants during cold weather. The trapping of heat that occurs during the greenhouse effect is also a good thing. In fact, it is not only good, it is necessary! Without it, our Earth would be a sphere of ice.

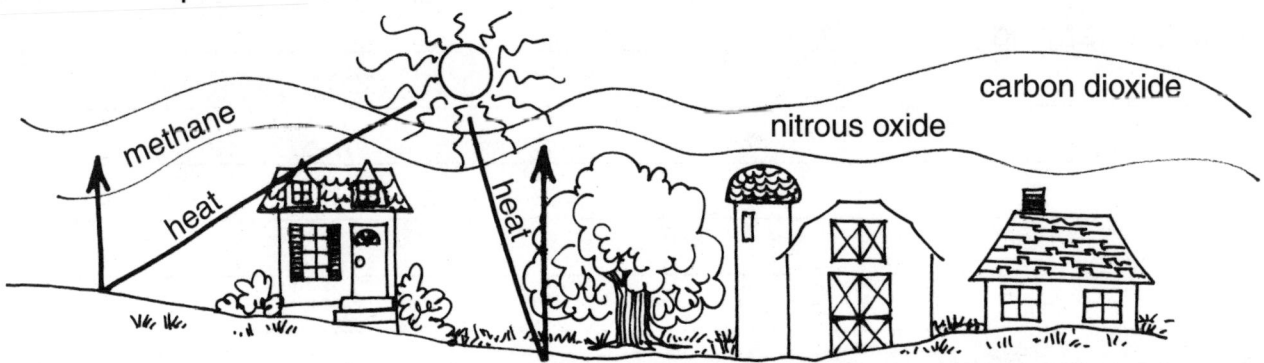

There is a problem with the greenhouse effect, however. The amount of gases we send into the air has increased. These gases include **carbon dioxide** from burning fossil fuels such as coal, gas, and oil to run factories and cars, and **methane**, which comes from burning trees and other vegetation. (Burning or cutting down trees without replanting them is known as **deforestation**.) **Nitrous oxide** is another gas which contributes to the greenhouse effect. It comes from sources such as some fertilizers and from burning fossil fuels and vegetation. Because the amount of gases in the atmosphere is increasing, the layer above us has grown thicker. This causes more heat to become trapped between the earth and the layer of gases. Scientists believe this is causing **global warming,** the warming of the earth.

1. In your own words, explain how the greenhouse effect occurs. _____

   _____

   _____

   _____

2. Describe two things you believe would help reduce the amount of gas we are sending into the air. _____

   _____

   _____

   _____

© 1999 McDONALD PUBLISHING CO.   ENVIRONMENTAL ISSUES

Name _____

Slowing Global Warming

Global warming is caused by the "greenhouse effect," the method by which the earth is heated by the sun. Unfortunately, the increased amount of gases we are sending into the air seems to have trapped too much heat. This is leading to a warming of the earth which scientists believe could cause many problems.

1. Brainstorm possible problems which might result from the warming of Earth.

   _____
   _____

One possible problem could be a change in weather patterns. The result could be an increase in hurricanes and monsoons as well as damaging floods and mud slides. As the earth gets warmer, the polar ice caps in the Arctic and Antarctic melt, causing a rise in sea level. This in turn causes flooding in low-lying areas, as well as the loss of coastal land. The Cape Hatteras Lighthouse in North Carolina was moved farther inland for this reason.

One way to slow global warming is to reduce the amount of gases we send into the air, especially from industry. In poorer countries, much coal is still burned to generate power. This causes a great amount of carbon dioxide to enter the atmosphere. Other methods must be used regularly worldwide to make a difference.

2. Write ideas for ways to reduce the amount of gas created by the following:

   A. Burning gas in cars _____
   _____

   B. Burning trash _____
   _____

   C. Burning leaves _____
   _____

   D. Using natural gas to heat houses _____
   _____

3. Explain how you might be able to tell if your local weather was being affected by global warming.

   _____
   _____

© 1999 McDONALD PUBLISHING CO.   ENVIRONMENTAL ISSUES

Name _____

What Is Ozone?

Ozone is a form of oxygen found high in the upper layers of the earth's atmosphere. There it forms a protective screen against the sun's radiation. Without this gas, our planet would have no protection from harmful radiation from the sun.

The earth's atmosphere has four levels.

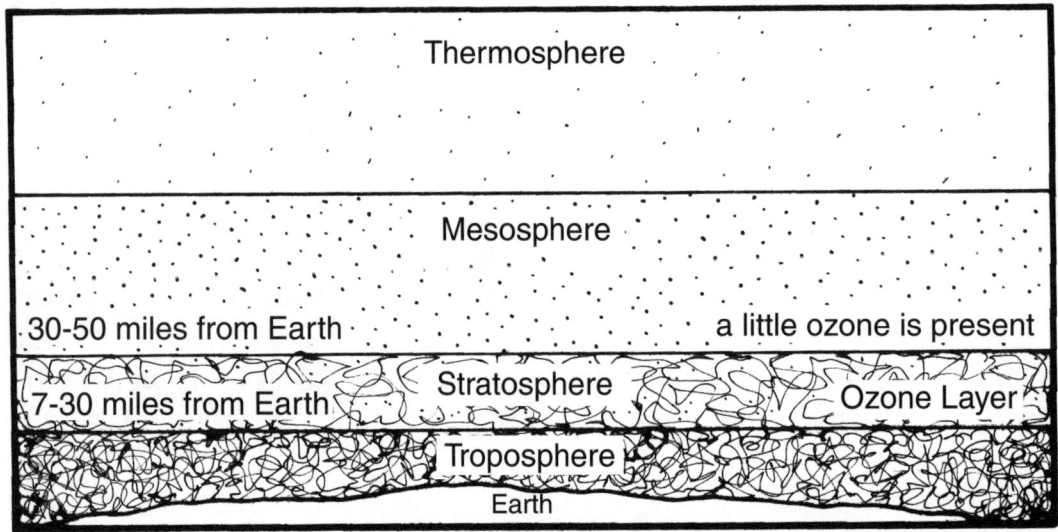

The protective layer of ozone in the stratosphere allows for life on Earth. **Ozone depletion**, the thinning of the ozone layer, can create holes in the shield of ozone which allow harmful ultraviolet rays to reach the earth. These rays may do damage to human skin, eyes, and possibly even our immune systems, which help us fight off diseases. Food sources for other animals could also be damaged.

A decrease in the ozone layer is a problem, but so is an increase in the layer. If too many gases from the earth, such as the carbon monoxide from car exhaust and hydrocarbons from industries, are added to the ozone there is a buildup of gases which we refer to as smog. This type of ozone pollution is harmful to all living things and also causes damage to paint, rubber, and the surfaces of buildings and other objects.

1. What problems might a decrease or increase in ozone cause? _____
   _____
   _____

2. In the box to the right, create a diagram that shows what happens when there is an increase or decrease in the amount of ozone.

© 1999 McDONALD PUBLISHING CO.   ENVIRONMENTAL ISSUES

Name _____

The Tree of Life

1. How important is a tree? On the lines below, write all the ways trees are useful to the earth and to the plants and animals that live there.

   _____
   _____
   _____
   _____
   _____

We need a small amount of carbon dioxide to live, but too much of it causes a warming of the earth. One of the most important jobs a tree does for the earth is to remove carbon dioxide from the air. All green plants convert carbon dioxide into the food plants use for growth and energy. The larger the plant, the more carbon dioxide it uses. A tree is a large plant which grows for many years. During its lifetime, a tree stores vast amounts of carbon in its tissues after removing it from the air we breathe.

Trees in our forests are being cut down each day. The wood is used to make such products as lumber, paper, or cardboard. Many companies plant new trees in place of the old forests.

2. Work with a partner to write the advantages of replanting forests once the trees are cut down. _____
   _____

   Will replanting forests keep the amount of carbon dioxide the same? _____
   Why or why not? _____
   _____

Humans are sending far too much carbon dioxide into the air. The more trees we plant on Earth, the more carbon dioxide will be removed from the air. There is room for planting trees near many homes and businesses in our country. With a partner, create a slogan (a short, catchy phrase) urging people to plant trees.

© 1999 McDONALD PUBLISHING CO.   ENVIRONMENTAL ISSUES

Name _____

Trees as Buffers

A buffer is something that protects something else from a strong force. Your bike helmet acts as a buffer to protect your head in case of a fall. On the lines below, list two other examples of buffers and write what they protect.

1. _____
2. _____

Bodies of water need buffers to protect them from damage caused by nature and humans. Trees are natural buffers that protect water. Erosion is the wearing away of land. Trees can help prevent erosion because their roots dig deep into the ground and help to hold the soil in place. The more trees there are in an area, the more roots there are to help prevent erosion. When rainwater runs across the land, the soil stays in place rather than traveling with the rainwater into nearby lakes or rivers.

As natural areas are destroyed to make way for construction, waterways are losing their buffer zones. When rain falls on grassy or forested areas, the water travels into the ground to provide water for plants and trees. When paved areas, such as sidewalks and parking lots, are created, however, the water flows across the areas rather than seeping into the soil. Oil and gasoline from cars as well as trash, detergents and other household chemicals, and dirt from exhaust ride on the surface of paved areas and are carried into nearby bodies of water every time it rains. This is a major source of water pollution. Many cities and towns with watershed property are now learning to restrict new construction in these areas to protect bodies of water and the organisms that live in or around them.

3. What is a buffer? _____

4. How might pollutants entering the water from paved surfaces affect fish and wildlife?
   _____
   _____
   _____

5. How do trees act as buffers in controlling erosion?
   _____
   _____

6. Use your telephone directory to locate the name, address, and telephone number of one local agency to whom you could write for more information on trees as buffers.
   _____
   _____

© 1999 McDONALD PUBLISHING CO.   ENVIRONMENTAL ISSUES

Name _____

Tropical Rain Forests

Tropical rain forests are found along the equator in South America, Latin America, Australia, southeast Asia, and central Africa. They cover about 4 million square miles of Earth's surface.

Rain forests provide a unique environment. They are lush and moist because they collect large amounts of moisture in the gigantic canopy. The canopy also serves as a huge umbrella. The trees in a rain forest help prevent soil erosion and flooding by holding soil in place and absorbing great amounts of water.

Although rain forests contain only about 6-7% of the world's land, they contain almost half of the world's animal and plant species. The rain forest is home to jaguars, lizards, rodents, monkeys, birds, sloths, frogs, ocelots, tapirs, bats, and many, many other animals. The animal and plant species in rain forests are so plentiful that many of them have not even been identified.

Unfortunately, there are only about half the amount of tropical rain forests as existed in 1950. The rain forests are disappearing so fast, in fact, that some species may vanish without our ever knowing of them.

Rain forests help people in many ways. Ingredients for many medicines, including digitalis for heart failure, come from the tropical rain forests. Tropical rain forests help to clean our air. They provide much of the oxygen in the world and take in great amounts of carbon dioxide.

Now valuable rain forests are disappearing. The trees are being cut down by loggers and cleared by farmers to raise cattle or crops. In some cases the clearing of land and raising of crops on rain forest land is vital for the survival of the people there. However, many farmers there use the soil until it is no longer fertile, then they clear additional land. It is important for them to learn ways to reuse cleared land rather than clearing additional land.

1. List two important things tropical rain forests contribute to the world. _____
   _____
   _____

2. List two bad effects the destruction of the rain forests could cause. _____
   _____
   _____

With a small group, develop a television advertisement educating the public on the value of the tropical rain forests and urging people to help care for them. Be prepared to act out the ad in front of your classmates.

© 1999 McDONALD PUBLISHING CO.   ENVIRONMENTAL ISSUES

Gifts from the Rain Forest

Tropical rain forests provide humans with many different types of products. The puzzle below contains the names of ten products humans receive from the rain forest. The words may be written horizontally (across) or vertically (up and down). Look carefully at the puzzle then circle the names of the products. While you're at it, see if you can find the names of the three layers of a rain forest too!

```
R Q X C Q A D F E R W A I E P S
Y W Z U W S S M E D I C I N E S
I E A N C O F F E E O R U A P D
O B S D E D A G Z T I E L I P F
K A P E A N U T S Y A O T R E G
F N D R R M O I S T F L O O R H
D A F S T F Z H Z L U P L M S J
S N G T Y G P I N E A P P L E S
C A N O P Y X J X M X U O Z A K
A S H R U H C O C O N U T S I L
S R J Y I J C J C N E L A U E M
H T K V O K V K V S C O I N U N
E Y L C I N N A M O N V B E O T
W U P B P L B L B U Z L X C V B
S I O N M M N M N K L N M L K J
```

"Save the Rain Forest" T-Shirt

One hectare of rain forest land (about 2.5 acres) may support 200 orchids, 10,000 mushrooms, 200 frogs, and a million ants. It could also support an anteater and two ocelots for quite a while. Unfortunately, humans are destroying many acres of rain forest land every minute. In fact, roughly 7,500 species of plants and animals are destroyed each year because of deforestation, the clearing of trees.

1. Using the numbers above, figure out how many species of plants and animals will be destroyed during the next five years if the deforestation rate remains the same. _____

2. If the deforestation rate were to decrease by half, how many species would be saved during a year? _____

At the rate the rain forests are disappearing, it is important for people to take notice of the destruction. It may soon be too late to save the millions of plant and animal species that call the tropical rain forest home.

Using the information on this page and on the page entitled "Tropical Rain Forests," create a T-shirt design that will call attention to the destruction of the rain forests. Try to make a creative and attractive design which will draw people's attention and inform them in some way.

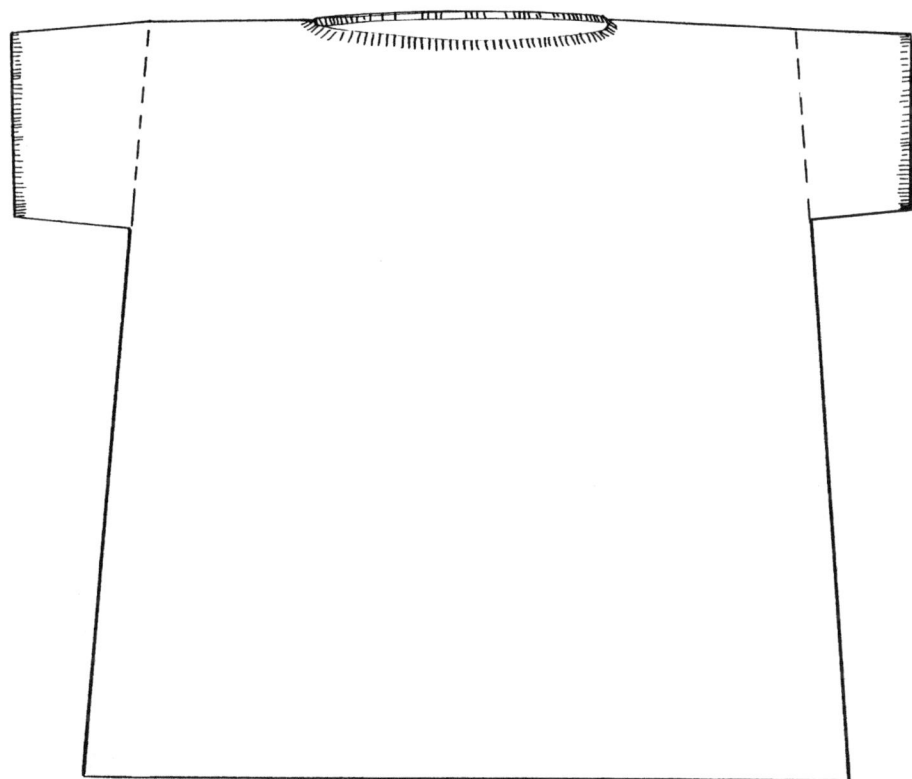

Proofread any written material on your T-shirt design. Share the design with a classmate and discuss ideas for improving it.

Name _____

Endangered Species

The ivory-billed woodpecker used to live in the lowlands and swamps in the southeastern part of the United States. It has not been spotted for many years and experts believe the bird may well be **extinct**, gone forever. This bird's habitat (home) was the forest, much of which has been destroyed by people either to build homes, to farm the land, or to sell the lumber.

This woodpecker is not the only species in danger of extinction. The shocking truth is that of the more than five million species of animals that have lived on Earth, at least one million species are already extinct. The main reason for this disappearance is that people are destroying the habitats of these animals. Other reasons for extinction include the killing of animals for their hides or tusks and the pollution of air and water.

While most people agree that it is important to prevent the extinction of species, there are other issues involved. For example, many people make a living cutting lumber in the large forests of the United States. These workers provide the wood that people need and use each day for paper, building materials, and much more. In some areas, the cutting of forests has caused species to become endangered. Biologists say it is dangerous to let even one species become extinct if we can prevent it. They argue that every species plays a role in the balance of nature, and that the extinction of one species can lead to the extinction of others.

Imagine that you have been asked to participate in a debate between people involved in the lumber industry and biologists who want to save forest-dwelling species from extinction.

1. First pretend to be a lumber worker. Write your reasons for wanting to continue to cut trees.

   _____
   _____
   _____
   _____

2. Now pretend you are a biologist. What are your reasons for wanting to protect forest-dwelling species?

   _____
   _____
   _____
   _____

Oil Spills

Oil, or petroleum, is an important source of energy for people around the world. Oil runs our vehicles and heats our homes and businesses. Many important products such as plastics and synthetic clothing are made from oil.

Problems arise when oil is spilled into our environment because oil is poisonous to living things. Oil spills usually occur when oil is being moved from one place to another. Most spills happen when the oil is being transported across the ocean in oil tankers. When a tanker runs aground, it can create a hole in the hull, the outer covering of the ship. The oil pours out of the hole into the sea. Because oil is lighter than water, it floats on top of the water. Oil floating on top of the water is called an **oil slick**.

At this point, depending on the amount of oil spilled, there is a potential disaster. Workers will be sent by the oil company as well as environmental groups to try and clean up the oil before it harms sea animals. Oil can poison animals. It can also coat birds' feathers and the fur of other sea animals. This coating destroys their ability to keep warm.

1. How would you go about cleaning up an oil spill before it reached the beaches?
___
___

There is no easy way to clean up an oil spill. While the oil is still on the water's surface, workers try to skim it off using boats equipped with special vacuums. Workers also construct fences to try to contain the oil.

2. What would you use in your cleanup effort after the oil reached the beaches?
___
___

Workers use rags and high-powered hoses, but in the end nature must do the final cleanup through evaporation and bacteria in the sea water which consumes some of the oil.

3. In a small group, list ways to prevent future oil spills.
___
___
___

Name _____

Space Junk

In 1983 as astronaut Sally Ride slept aboard the space shuttle *Challenger*, a fleck of paint smashed into the window. It left a crater the size of a pea. Because objects in space can travel at much higher speeds than those on Earth, the paint chip was traveling at about 1,400 miles per hour.

Unfortunately, that paint chip is not the only piece of junk in space. There are millions of pieces of junk zipping around in space at an average speed of 22,000 miles per hour.

1. Where do you think all this space junk came from? _____
_____

Until the 1940s no one had built a rocket strong enough to enter space. Before that time the only objects in space were natural ones. Once rockets and satellites were launched into space, the littering of space began with such items as particles of dust, flecks of paint, cast-off rocket stages, and tools dropped by astronauts.

Scientists believed that eventually gravity would pull the "space litter" down and the items would burn up in the atmosphere. Unfortunately, that is not happening nearly as fast as scientists expected. Right now, along with other types of space junk, there are more than 1,400 inactive man-made satellites orbiting the earth. More are launched every year.

2. Imagine that you are an astronaut. You are in space, trying to repair the outside of your spaceship. In the box above, draw a picture of yourself in your space suit with a variety of space junk interfering with your work.

3. Some people think a good way to escape the crowdedness and pollution on Earth is to live in a space station. What trash-related plans would have to be made before a large space station could be placed in space?
_____
_____

4. How would you protect the space station from the millions of pieces of speeding space junk which might hit the space station? _____
_____
_____

5. Since there is no life on the moon, what is your opinion of the idea to make the moon a trash dump for the earth? _____
_____

© 1999 McDONALD PUBLISHING CO.   ENVIRONMENTAL ISSUES

Name _____

The Truth About Trash

We hear a great deal about the need for recycling and about overfilled landfills. We read and hear the phrase "Save a Tree" quite often these days. But what can we really do to preserve the environment? Let's find out. Start by using the information in the box below to figure out the answers to the questions that follow.

A. It takes 17 trees to make one ton of paper. Those 17 trees can absorb 250 pounds of carbon dioxide from the air. Burning one ton of paper would create 1,500 pounds of carbon dioxide, contributing to the greenhouse gases that scientists are blaming for global warming.
B. Making one ton of recycled paper takes only 60% of the energy needed to make one ton of new paper.
C. Recycling a ton of steel saves 2,500 pounds of iron ore, 1,000 pounds of coal, and 40 pounds of limestone.
D. Throwing away a single aluminum can wastes about as much energy as it takes to run a TV for 3 hours.
E. The average person in the U.S. throws away 90,000 pounds of trash during a lifetime.
F. Recycling glass reduces mining waste by 80%, water use by 50%, and air pollution by 20%.

---

1. If everyone in your class, including the teacher, recycled 100 pounds of paper each year about how many trees would be saved? _____

2. Approximately how long could you run your television set with energy saved by recycling all the aluminum cans your family uses in one month? _____

3. How many pounds of trash will an average family of four throw away over their lifetimes? _____

4. How much iron ore is saved by recycling 4 tons of steel? _____

5. Which of the recycling ideas above do you think is the most likely to be used?
   _____
   Why? _____

6. Which of the above recycling ideas do you think is the least likely to be used?
   _____
   Why? _____

7. How important do you think saving space in the landfills is to our country?
   _____

8. What do you think will happen to the trash when all the landfills are filled? _____
   _____
   _____

© 1999 McDONALD PUBLISHING CO.   ENVIRONMENTAL ISSUES

Name _____

U.S. Recycling Report Card

How is the United States doing as a country in the fight against waste and overflowing landfills? Read the following facts. Then on the form below enter grades that reflect the progress of the United States in each area of recycling.

Facts

- About 2.5 million plastic bottles are used in the United States every hour. Despite the fact that plastic is very easy to recycle, Americans recycle very little of it.
- Enough aluminum is discarded in the United States to rebuild the nation's entire commercial airline fleet every three months.
- People in the U.S. are recycling enough steel annually to supply electricity to the city of Los Angeles for ten years.
- Each person in the U.S. throws away between four and six pounds of garbage each day.
- It is estimated that each year Americans dispose of 1 million tons of aluminum, 11 million tons of glass, and 14.5 million tons of paper products. Almost all of this could be recycled.
- One-third of all landfill space is taken up by plastics. Plastic materials may take anywhere from ten to one hundred years to decompose, and plastic-foam plates and cups and fast-food containers will never decompose.
- Some communities collect yard waste that can be composted (allowed to decay into a substance that enriches soil) to make fertilizer.
- Americans discard millions of disposable diapers each year. The diapers will take about 500 years to disintegrate.

Recycling Report Card

Name: *The United States*   Evaluator's Name: _____

Area	Grade (A, B, C, D, or F)	Comments
Paper		
Aluminum		
Plastics		
Yard Waste		
Glass		
Steel		
Diapers		

Suggestions for Improvement:

Name _____

Recycling Rangers

Imagine that you are traveling into the not-so-distant future. Landfills are a thing of the past and all people in the United States are required to recycle. Recycling Rangers have been assigned to help make sure that as many items as possible get recycled.

1. What would be the pros and cons of required, or mandatory, recycling? What are some alternatives?

   _____
   _____
   _____
   _____

2. Make a list of all the recyclable items in the following picture. After each item write a way it could be reused or recycled.

Item	How It Can Be Reused or Recycled

© 1999 McDONALD PUBLISHING CO.   ENVIRONMENTAL ISSUES

Name _____

The Earth's Friend or Foe?

The future condition of the earth will soon be in your hands. Will you conserve energy and natural resources or will you waste what is left of Earth's natural beauty and gifts? To find out how much you know about caring for the remaining resources of the earth, answer the following questions.

1. Does your neighborhood have a recycling program? _____

    If so, what do they accept? _____

2. Is there a recycling center or drop-off point near your house? _____

    If so, what do they accept? _____

3. What items does your family recycle? _____

4. How would buying in larger quantities in the grocery store cut down on waste and save your family money? _____

5. How can you avoid using paper or plastic shopping bags? _____

6. How can you reduce packaging waste when choosing items in the produce department? _____

7. How can fast-food restaurants cut down on packaging waste? _____

8. What can people do with unwanted toys or outgrown clothes in order to produce less waste? _____

9. What is a good way to reduce catalog and magazine pile-up? _____

10. In what other ways can you be a friend to the earth? _____

Smart Shopping for a Better World

Read this story of the Waster family's trip to the grocery store and see if you can discover several things about the trip which were not friendly to the environment.

The Wasters left all the lights on in the house as they piled into the car. They were driving to the grocery store four blocks away. Mrs. Waster pushed the cart through the produce aisle, tossing in a package of tomatoes. Mr. Waster bought three kinds of bagels and put each in a separate bag. Junior Waster picked out some paper plates and plastic utensils for his upcoming birthday party. Then he picked up his favorite individually wrapped cheese slices and took them to the cart. Sissie Waster bought six tiny cans of tuna. She knew it would take three larger cans to make one meal, but she liked the little cans. The Wasters loaded up on paper towels and napkins and then paid for the groceries. They all helped load the paper grocery bags into the car and headed for home.

Underline all of the environmentally unfriendly parts of the story above. Rewrite the story changing each unfriendly act into an Earth-friendly act.

_____
_____
_____
_____
_____
_____
_____
_____
_____

Name _____

Save Our Soil

Erosion is the wearing away of rock or soil. Soil is very important to life on Earth. Most plants cannot live without soil, and without plants, most animals could not live. It is important that we protect our topsoil from erosion. The effort to prevent erosion and protect soil is called **soil conservation**.

One of the major causes of erosion is rainwater. Rainwater can run across land, picking up soil and carrying it away. This can create serious problems for farmers who depend on fertile topsoil to provide nutrients to growing crops.

There are several ways farmers can work with the land in order to prevent erosion and conserve soil. One method of soil conservation is **terracing**. Water naturally carries soil downhill, but this can be prevented. When planting crops on sloped land, some farmers cut flat areas called terraces into the land, and then plant crops on them. The terraces hold water in place, preventing it from flowing downhill and carrying away valuable soil.

Contour plowing is another way to prevent erosion on sloping land. This involves plowing across a hill rather than up and down the hill. The ridges made by the plow run across the hill and hold water in place rather than letting it run downhill.

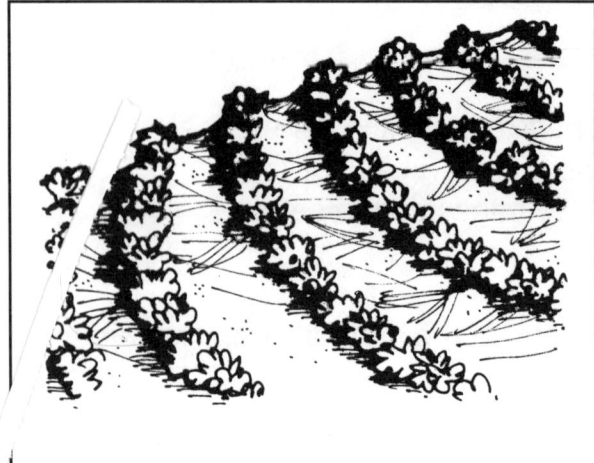

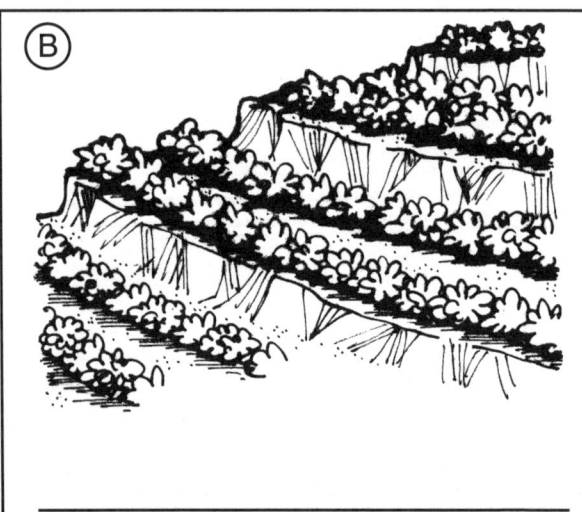

1. On the lines in the boxes to the left, label the two types of soil conservation shown.

2. The protection of soil is not the only type of conservation. There are many other types of conservation. On the lines below, write two ways you can help conserve water.

   _____
   _____
   _____
   _____
   _____

3. Describe one way that a farmer can prevent the soil erosion caused by wind when he or she is plowing or planting a field on an open prairie.

   _____
   _____
   _____
   _____

ENVIRONMENTAL ISSUES

Name _____

Creating Compost

Did you know that nature has its own way of making certain kinds of trash disappear? It's true! Composting is a way of creating natural fertilizer from organic trash (trash that was once alive) such as grass clippings, food scraps, plant parts, leaves, etc. Decomposers like bacteria help to make these materials decay into humus which adds nutrients to the soil. Nutrients help plants to grow. Many gardeners use compost to fertilize their gardens, loosen the soil, and help the soil stay damp.

Composting helps decrease the amount of trash sent to landfills. In fact, many communities require residents to separate materials such as twigs, leaves, and grass clippings from other types of trash. The natural materials can then be composted rather than sent to landfills. This procedure can decrease the amount of landfill material by as much as twenty percent.

In a compost pile, organic trash is packed into layers. A thin layer of soil or manure is placed between each thick layer of trash. Often the layers are dampened to speed up the decay. The materials are also mixed occasionally to allow oxygen to reach the decomposers. After several months, the trash will have turned into rich, dark humus and can be used to provide plants with nutrients. This process can be done by individuals or by composting companies that compost large amounts of waste.

Write true *or* false *before each statement below about composting.*

1. _____ All types of trash can be composted.
2. _____ Composting can help reduce the amount of trash sent to landfills.
3. _____ Oxygen is an important part of the composting process.
4. _____ Materials called decomposers help to break down organic trash.
5. _____ The composting process takes only a few days.
6. _____ Composting would not work without decomposers.
7. _____ Humus is a type of decomposer used in composting.

8. Circle the materials below that are organic and could be placed in a home compost pile.

fallen leaves	glass jars	twigs
coffee grounds	grass clippings	aluminum cans
beans	plastic wrap	hay
lettuce	tin foil	tree bark

© 1999 McDONALD PUBLISHING CO.   ENVIRONMENTAL ISSUES

Name _____

Environmental Jobs

During the last few decades there has been more and more emphasis on the need to protect our environment. Problems such as global warming, ozone depletion, and others have created a need for more environmental specialists. This is good news for people who want to make a living trying to protect and improve the world around them.

There are enough environmental careers to fill an entire book, but here are descriptions of five of them:

Ecologist: Ecologists study natural history and are interested in how a species develops and the relationships among different animals and/or insects. Most ecologists teach at universities and conduct research.

Environmental Toxicologist: A toxicologist is an environmental chemist who performs tests on animals to find out how they are affected by radiation, poisons, gases, pesticides, and other substances. A toxicologist might be brought in after an oil spill to determine the effects of oil on the area wildlife.

Environmental Engineer: This type of engineer leads an active life and is involved in service to the community in a variety of ways. He or she may develop a plan to repair deteriorating infrastructure such as sewers or bridge supports or educate a community in earthquake preparedness. These engineers are also called upon to assess the impact of proposed power plants on an area.

Industrial Hygienist: The industrial hygienist works in industries to try to eliminate occupational health hazards and diseases. He or she would judge the effects of chemicals on the people who work with them. Job-related stress is another concern of the industrial hygienist.

Forester: Just as the name implies, this job concerns the forest and everything about it, including trees, wildlife, fish, protection from insects and diseases, etc. The forester plants trees, fights fires, and works to keep forests beautiful.

1. Which of the environmental jobs described above would you be most interested in and why? _____
   _____

2. Which of the jobs above would you be least interested in and why? _____
   _____

3. On the back of this paper, write two questions you would ask someone in each of these fields.

Name _____

Energy Store

We talk a lot about conserving our natural resources. We know that our fossil fuels (oil, coal, natural gas) are nonrenewable. We cannot simply make more of these fuels and it takes a very long time for these fuels to form naturally. It is important that we find ways to conserve these resources.

Many communities are considering programs to encourage people to conserve and recycle. Imagine a program that involves points that can be used to buy energy products. Each household is given 1,000 points per month to spend on one month's energy needs. The point value of various activities is listed below.

Energy Products or Activities	Point Value	Points Spent or Gained
Gasoline for car	– 500	_____
Carpooling (school or work)	+ 50	_____
Heat for home	– 250	_____
Daily newspaper	– 25	_____
Swimming pool	– 75	_____
Vegetable garden	+ 25	_____
Using fireplace	– 50	_____
Buying frozen foods	– 25	_____
Trash pick-up	– 25	_____
Air conditioning home	– 75	_____
Not recycling	– 100	_____
Recycling	+ 25	_____
Sprinkling system	– 50	_____
Using paper bags	– 25	_____

Imagine that you are in charge of a household. Determine what energy products or activities you will use during the month of August. Fill in the chart to show how you will spend your 1,000 points. Note that you may acquire additional points by having a vegetable garden, carpooling, or recycling.

1. What other items should be added to the chart that would use up or add points?
   _____
   _____

2. Imagine you have been asked to evaluate this new program. Would you recommend it? Why or why not? _____
   _____
   _____

© 1999 McDONALD PUBLISHING CO.   ENVIRONMENTAL ISSUES

Name _____

The Wonders of Water

Water is vital to life on Earth. People drink it, cook in it, bathe with it, and use it to grow crops. Water plays an important part in most manufacturing processes too. Animals, of course, also need water in order to live.

Water covers nearly three-fourths of Earth's surface, but only three percent of all that water is freshwater. The rest of the water is saltwater. Three-fourths of the freshwater that does exist on Earth is frozen in glaciers and polar ice caps. That leaves a small amount of freshwater available to people, animals, and industries around the world. Obviously it is important that humans protect and conserve water.

Protecting water is a big job. Many lakes and rivers have been polluted by trash and chemicals. Water pollution may be as small as an aluminum can left by a careless beach visitor, or as large as an oil spill created by a tanker. No matter how the pollution occurs, people and their governments must take steps to reduce the amount of pollution that reaches streams, lakes, and rivers.

It is also important to conserve water (use less water). Each person in the United States uses roughly 80 gallons of water each day. There are several ways people can cut back on the amount of water they use. For example, people can water their lawns early in the day or late in the day when less evaporation occurs. They can fix leaky pipes and faucets, and wash their cars only when necessary.

1. List three things you could do to reduce the amount of water you use on a typical day.

   _____

   _____

   _____

2. Create a pie chart under each heading to show the percents of each type of water. Be sure to label the sections of your pie chart.

Water on Earth
Freshwater vs. Saltwater

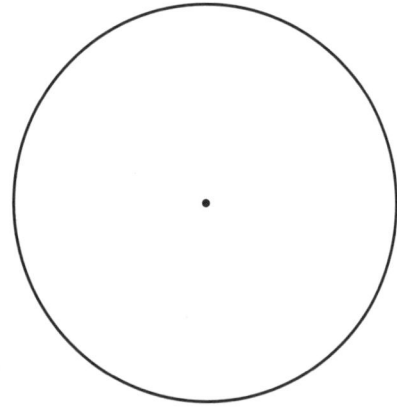

Freshwater on Earth
Frozen vs. Usable

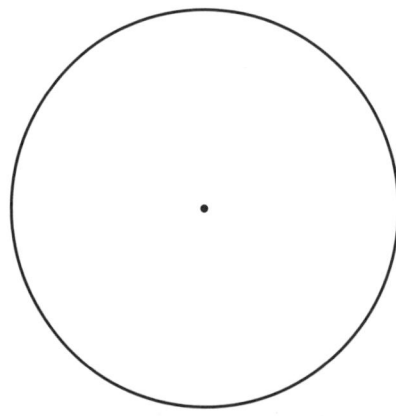

Name _____

It's a Start

You know it is important that we do more to protect the environment. However, you may not realize that many steps have already been taken to improve the world around us. Here are some of them:

In June of 1998 Suriname, a country in South America, announced that it would permanently protect 4 million acres of rain forest land.

Automobile manufacturers are working to produce cars that give off smaller amounts of carbon dioxide and other gases that create smog.

Many communities are requiring residents to separate organic waste from other materials that will be sent to landfills. The organic waste is then used to create compost.

People in every state can see endangered species that have recovered or that are increasing in number. In recent years some animals were removed from the endangered species list because they are no longer in danger of disappearing from the earth.

Many people have made recycling part of their daily routine. By 1990 people were recycling nearly two-thirds of aluminum cans.

"Reduce. Reuse. Recycle." has become a well-known environmental slogan. Think of items you use every day that could be reduced, reused, or recycled. List as many of them as possible on the lines below.

Reduce _____
_____
_____

Reuse _____
_____
_____

Recycle _____
_____
_____

What Can One Person Do?

Your teacher has informed you about many issues in the environment. However, there are many other sources you can use to learn about the environment. On the lines below, list as many sources of environmental information as you can.

_____
_____
_____

Did you know that you and your classmates can be an important source of environmental information? Here are some ideas to get you started.

Make and Distribute Posters

Choose an issue related to your school or community. For example, there may be trash that needs to be picked up around your school or you may want to start a recycling program in your community. Decide on a theme—a "title" that will appear on all the posters. Work together with other students, teachers, and the principal at your school to gather materials and volunteers to make posters. When the posters are made, have volunteers post them around the school and community. (Be sure to get permission first.)

Create an idea and design your own poster dealing with an environmental issue in the box to the right.

Write a Grant

A grant is a request for money that is written to a company or organization. Many companies and organizations donate money to worthwhile environmental causes, especially when students will use the money to do community service. There are many companies and organizations listed on the Internet that would welcome student-written grants.

On the lines below, list ways you could use $5,000 in grant money to improve the environment in your community.

_____
_____
_____

Name _____

Environmental Sentences

The sentences that follow are designed to increase your awareness of environmental issues and encourage you to make choices that help preserve the environment and make the world a better place for future generations. Complete the sentences thoughtfully and completely.

1. The best way to deal with people who litter is _____ _____

2. One way I can help conserve natural resources like fossil fuels is to _____ _____

3. The environmental issue I am most concerned about is _____ _____

4. It is important for people to realize that the earth _____ _____

5. If ozone depletion lets in rays from the sun that cause skin cancer _____ _____

6. If I were captain of a tanker carrying oil across the sea I would _____ _____

7. I think recycling is _____

8. Some people don't think space junk affects them because _____ _____

9. If we don't conserve energy _____

10. If I were living in the rain forest I would _____

11. The way I feel about using cloth napkins and diapers instead of using disposable ones is _____

12. Global warming is probably _____

13. The first thing I would tell my own child about the environment is _____

14. One thing I could give up to help save the environment is _____

After everyone has completed the sentences, form a group with three or four other students and discuss your answers. Choose a topic on which your group has strong opinions and prepare a short speech about that topic. Either select one member of your group to give the speech or divide it into equal parts and give it as a group. Be prepared to answer questions about your topic.

© 1999 McDONALD PUBLISHING CO.

Environment Crossword Puzzle

Use your knowledge of environmental issues to complete this crossword puzzle.

Across
1. The leafy top layer of a rain forest
3. a gas produced by plants during photosynthesis
5. The lower part of a rain forest is known as the moist _____.
8. a colorless gas given off by humans and absorbed by plants (2 words)
10. Inactive satellites orbiting Earth are litter in _____.
12. a study of the relationships between organisms and their environment
14. to reuse an item or make it into something new in order to conserve resources
15. the world around us
16. a combination of *smoke* and *fog*
17. the part of a rain forest beneath the canopy and above the moist floor

Down
2. a form of oxygen responsible for blocking harmful ultraviolet rays
4. The belief that the earth is becoming warmer because gases are trapping the sun's heat is called _____ warming.
6. Animals in danger of becoming extinct are called _____ species.
7. A tropical woodland containing evergreens that receives a great deal of rain is called a _____. (2 words)
9. Oil floating on top of water is referred to as an _____. (2 words)
11. An animal group that no longer exists on Earth is called _____.
13. grass clippings, leaves, etc. that are allowed to decay to form a substance that enriches the soil

© 1999 McDONALD PUBLISHING CO.   ENVIRONMENTAL ISSUES

Name _____

Environmental Glossary

- **atmosphere** – the air surrounding a planet.
- **canopy** – the leafy top layer of the rain forest formed by the gigantic treetops.
- **carbon dioxide** – a common carbon compound present in the atmosphere in increasingly large amounts and caused by human activities such as burning fossil fuels.
- **climate** – the average weather conditions found in a certain area over a long period of time.
- **compost** – grass clippings, plant parts, leaves, etc. that have been allowed to decay into a substance that enriches the soil.
- **conservation** – measures taken to preserve natural resources such as fossil fuels and forests.
- **deforestation** – the clearing of forests.
- **drought** – a long period of time without sufficient precipitation.
- **ecologist** – a scientist who studies the relationships between organisms and their environments.
- **environment** – all things that surround us: the air, land, water, plants, and animals.
- **erosion** – the washing away of soil by wind, running water, or glacial activity.
- **extinct** – died out over millions of years, as in the dinosaur.
- **fossil fuels** – oil, coal, and natural gas formed from the remains of organisms that lived millions of years ago including the dinosaur.
- **global warming** – the belief of many scientists that the earth is warming up because of increased amounts of gases in the atmosphere which are trapping the sun's heat.
- **greenhouse effect** – the trapping of heat in the atmosphere by water vapor and gases (especially carbon dioxide) which act like a greenhouse.
- **groundwater** – water from the atmosphere which circulates below the surface of the earth.
- **landfill** – a place where solid waste is dumped
- **mesosphere** – the layer of atmosphere above the stratosphere, extending from a height of 30 miles to about 50 miles above the earth's surface.
- **methane** – a hydrocarbon gas that is given off by the decomposition of organic matter such as dead animals.
- **nitrogen** – the most plentiful gas in the atmosphere.
- **oil spill** – an accident, usually to an oil tanker or pipeline, causing vast amounts of oil to spill into the sea or ground.
- **overpopulation** – having too many people on the earth.

Environmental Glossary (continued)

- **oxygen** – the second most plentiful gas on the earth, the one necessary for plants and animals to breathe.
- **ozone** – a form of oxygen responsible for blocking harmful ultraviolet rays.
- **ozone depletion** – the thinning of ozone which prevents harmful ultraviolet rays from damaging skin, eyes, etc.
- **pollution** – anything which contaminates air, water, or land, making it harmful to use them.
- **satellite** – an object in orbit around another larger object.
- **recycling** – reusing items (or using materials to make new items) in order to conserve resources.
- **smog** – a mixture of smoke and fog.
- **solar energy** – energy obtained from the sun.
- **space junk** – pieces of man-made debris in space circling our planet.
- **tropical rain forests** – forests along the equator which are home to half the world's plant and animal species. These forests clean the air and protect the soil.
- **troposphere** – the lowest layer (about 7 miles high) of the earth's atmosphere.
- **understory** – the part of the rain forest beneath the canopy and above the moist floor.
- **ultraviolet radiation** – an invisible form of short-wave radiation given off by the sun. It is harmful to exposed organisms.

Choose two terms from the Environmental Glossary and write a paragraph about each explaining in detail what you know about the subject.

1. _____

2. _____